Andrew Dickson White

Fiat Money in France

How it Came, What it Brought, and How it Ended

Andrew Dickson White

Fiat Money in France
How it Came, What it Brought, and How it Ended

ISBN/EAN: 9783744723725

Printed in Europe, USA, Canada, Australia, Japan

Cover: Foto ©ninafisch / pixelio.de

More available books at **www.hansebooks.com**

FIAT MONEY IN FRANCE

HOW IT CAME, WHAT IT BROUGHT
AND HOW IT ENDED

BY

ANDREW D. WHITE

NEW YORK
D. APPLETON AND COMPANY
1896

INTRODUCTION.

As far back as just before the civil war I made a large collection of documents which appeared during the French Revolution, including newspapers, reports, speeches, pamphlets, and illustrative material of every sort, and especially specimens of nearly all the issues of paper money then made—from notes of ten thousand francs to those of one sou.

Upon this material, mainly, was based a course of lectures then given to my university students, and among these lectures one on Paper Money Inflation in France.

This was given simply because it showed one important line of facts in that great struggle; and I recall, as if it were yesterday, my feeling of regret at being obliged to bestow so much care and labor upon a subject to all appearance so utterly devoid of practical value. I am sure that it never occurred either to my students or myself that it could have any bearing on our own country. It certainly never entered into our minds that any such folly as that exhibited in those French documents of the eighteenth century would eventually find supporters in the United States of the nineteenth.

Some years later, when there began to be proposals for large issues of paper, I wrought some of the facts thus collected into a speech in the Senate of the State of New York, showing the need of especial care in such dealings with financial necessities.

In 1876, during the "greenback craze," General Garfield and Mr. S. B. Chittenden, both members of the House of Representatives at that time, asked me to read a paper on the same general subject before an audience of Senators and Representatives of both parties in Washington. This I did, and also gave it before an assemblage of New York men of business at the Union League Club.

Various editions of the paper were afterward published, among these one for campaign purposes, and it now appears that there is a demand for another, and that it may be of use in showing to what folly, cruelty, wrong, and ruin the passion for fiat money may lead.

There is perhaps a special reason for issuing this new edition, in the fact that the principle involved in the proposed unlimited coinage of silver in the United States is, at bottom, identical with the idea which led to that fearful wreck of public and private prosperity in France.

And there is an added reason in the fact that the utterances of the Chicago nominee and of the Populist platform point clearly and unmistakably to unlimited issues of paper money hereafter. Whatever so-called "Democrats" may intend at present, their candidate and his Populist supporters are logical enough to see that it would be inconsistent to stop at the unlimited issue of silver dollars, which really cost something, when they can issue unlimited paper dollars which virtually cost nothing.

In thus exhibiting facts which Lord Bacon would have recognized as confirming his theory of The Possible Insanity of Great States, it is but just to acknowledge that the French proposal was vastly more sane than that now made in our own country. The French issues of paper rested not merely " on the will of a free people," but on more than one third of the entire landed property of France ; on the very choicest of real estate in city and country—the confiscated estates of the Church and the fugitive aristocracy—with power to use the paper thus issued in purchasing this real property at very moderate prices. Our proposed unlimited issue of silver rests on we know not what; and the proposed issue of paper rests solely upon the judgment, the will, and the schemes for political success or personal gain of those Populist financiers who shall be put in control at Washington, and who will doubtless be astute enough to see and to use the enormous possibilities for stockjobbing and gambling in values which will accrue to those who, by controlling the issues of the circulating medium, can raise or depress the price of every share of stock, every bond, every yard of every fabric, every ounce of every commodity within the United States.

I have taken all pains to be exact, giving the authority for every important statement, and now leave the whole matter with my readers.

ANDREW D. WHITE.

ITHACA, N. Y., *August 8, 1896.*

FIAT MONEY IN FRANCE.

HOW IT CAME, WHAT IT BROUGHT, AND HOW IT ENDED.*

NEAR the end of the year 1789 the French nation found itself in deep financial embarrassment: there was a heavy debt and a serious deficit.

The vast reforms of that year, though a lasting blessing politically, were a temporary evil financially. There was a general want of confidence in business circles; capital had shown its proverbial timidity by retiring out of sight as far as possible; but little money was in circulation; throughout the land was temporary stagnation.

Statesmanlike measures, careful watching, and wise management, would doubtless have led, ere long, to a return of confidence, a reappearance of money, and resumption of business;† but this in-

---

* A paper read before a meeting of Senators and members of the House of Representatives of both political parties, at Washington, April 12th; and before the Union League Club, at New York, April 13, 1876.

† For proof that the financial situation of France at that time was by no means hopeless, see Storch, Économie Politique, vol. iv, p. 159.

volved waiting, self-denial, and self-sacrifice; and
thus far in human history those are the rarest
products of an improved political condition. Few
nations, up to this time, have been able to exercise
these virtues; and France was not then one of
those few.

There was a general looking about for some short
road to prosperity; ere long, the idea was set afloat
that the great want of the country was more of the
circulating medium; and this was speedily followed
by calls for an issue of paper money. The Minister
of Finance at this period was Necker. In financial
ability he was acknowledged among the great bankers of Europe; but he had something more than
financial ability: he had a deep feeling of patriotism and a high sense of personal honor. The difficulties in his way were great, but he steadily endeavored to keep France faithful to those financial
principles which the general experience of modern
times had established as the only path to national
safety. As difficulties arose, the National Assembly
drew away from him, and soon came among the
members muttered praises of paper money; members like Allarde and Gouy held it up as a panacea
—as a way of "securing resources without paying
interest." This was echoed outside; the journalist
Loustalot caught it up and proclaimed its beauties;

Marat, in his newspaper, also joined the cries against
Necker, picturing him—a man who gave up health
and fortune for the sake of France—as a wretch
seeking only to enrich himself from the public
purse.

Against the tendency to the issue of irredeemable paper Necker contended as best he might. He
knew well to what it had always led, even when surrounded by the most skillful guarantees. Among
those who struggled to aid him outside the National
Assembly was Bergasse, a deputy from Lyons,
whose pamphlets against an irredeemable paper
exerted, perhaps, a wider influence than any others;
parts of them seem fairly inspired. Any one to-day
reading his prophecies of the evils sure to follow
such a currency would certainly ascribe to him a
miraculous foresight, were it not so clear that this
prophetic power was simply due to a knowledge of
natural laws.* But the current was too strong; on
the 19th of April, 1790, the Finance Committee of
the Assembly reported that " the people demand a
new circulating medium "; that " the circulation of

---

* See Buchez and Roux, Histoire Parlémentaire de la Révolution Française, vol. iii, pp. 364, 365; also p. 405.

For pamphlet itself, see the A. D. White Collection in the
Library of Cornell University; for the effect produced by it, see
Challamel, Les Français sous la Révolution. Also De Goncourt,
La Société Française pendant la Révolution.

paper money is the best of operations"; that "it is
the most free because it reposes on the will of the
people"; that "it will bind the interests of the citizens to the public good."

The report appealed to the patriotism of the
French people with the following exhortation:
"Let us show to Europe that we understand our
own resources; let us immediately take the broad
road to our liberation, instead of dragging ourselves
along the tortuous and obscure paths of fragmentary
loans:" it concluded by recommending an issue of
paper money, carefully guarded, to the amount of
four hundred million francs. The next day the debate begins. M. Martineau is loud and long for
paper money. His only fear is, that the committee
has not authorized enough of it; he declares that
business is stagnant, and that the sole cause is a
want of more of the circulating medium; that
paper money ought to be made a legal tender; that
the Assembly should rise above the prejudices
which the failure of John Law's paper money had
caused. Like every supporter of irredeemable
paper money before or since, he seems to think that
the laws of Nature have changed since previous disastrous issues. He says: "Paper money under a
despotism is dangerous; it favors corruption; but
in a nation constitutionally governed, which itself

takes care of the emission of its notes, which deter-
mines their number and use, that danger no longer
exists." He insists that John Law's notes at first
restored prosperity, but that the wretchedness and
wrong they caused resulted from their overissue,
and that such an overissue is possible only under a
despotism.*

M. de la Rochefoucauld gives his opinion that
" the assignats will draw specie out of the coffers
where it is now hoarded." †

On the other hand, Cazalès and Maury showed
that the result could only be disastrous. Never,
perhaps, did a political prophecy meet with more
exact fulfillment in every line than the terrible picture drawn in one of Cazalès's speeches in this debate. Still the current ran stronger and stronger ;
Petion made a brilliant oration in favor of the report, and Necker's influence and experience were
gradually worn away.

But mingled with the financial argument was a
very strong political argument. The nation had
just taken as its own the vast real property of the
French Church, the pious accumulations of thirteen
hundred years. There were princely estates in the

---

* See Moniteur, sitting of April 10, 1790.
† Ibid., sitting of April 15, 1790.

country, sumptuous palaces and conventual buildings in the towns; these formed about one third of
the entire real property of France, and amounted in
value to about four thousand million francs, yielding
a yearly income of about two hundred millions.*
By one sweeping stroke all this had become the
property of the nation; never, apparently, did a nation secure a more solid basis for a great financial
future.

There were two great reasons why French statesmen desired speedily to sell these lands. First, a
financial reason—to obtain money to relieve the
Government. Secondly, a political reason—to get
this land distributed among the thrifty middle classes,
and so to commit them to the Revolution and to the
Government which gave their title.

It was urged, then, that the issue of four hundred millions of paper would give the treasury
something to pay out immediately, and relieve the
national necessities; that, having been put into circulation, this paper money would stimulate business;
that it would give to all capitalists, large or small,
the means for buying of the nation the ecclesiastical
real estate, and that from the proceeds of this real

---

* See De Nervo, Finances Françaises, vol. ii, p. 236; also
Alison, vol. i.

estate the nation would again obtain new funds for new necessities : never was theory more seductive both to financiers and statesmen.

But it would be a great mistake to suppose that the statesmen of France, or the French people, were ignorant of the dangers of issuing irredeemable paper money. No matter how skillfully the bright side of such a currency was exhibited, all thoughtful men in France knew something of its dark side. They knew too well, from that fearful experience in John Law's time, the difficulties and dangers of a currency not based upon specie. They had then learned how easy it is to issue it ; how difficult it is to check an overissue ; how seductively it leads to the absorption of the means of the workingmen and men of small fortunes ; how surely it impoverishes all men living on fixed incomes, salaries, or wages ; how it creates on the ruins of the prosperity of all workingmen a small class of debauched speculators, the most injurious class that a nation can harbor, more injurious, indeed, than professional criminals whom the law recognizes and can throttle ; how it stimulates overproduction at first, and leaves every industry flaccid afterward ; how it breaks down thrift, and develops political and social immorality. All this France had been thoroughly taught by experience. Many then living had felt the results of

such an experiment—the issues of paper money under John Law, a man who is to this day acknowledged one of the most ingenious financiers the world
has ever known; and there were then sitting in the
National Assembly of France many who owed the
poverty of their families to those issues of paper.
Hardly a man in the country who had not heard
those who issued it cursed as the authors of the
most frightful catastrophe France had then known.*
It was no mere attempt at theatrical display, but a
natural impulse, which led a thoughtful statesman,
during this debate, to hold up in the Assembly a
piece of paper money, and to declare that it was
moistened with the blood and tears of their fathers.
And it would also be a mistake to suppose that the
National Assembly which discussed this matter was
composed of mere wild revolutionists; no supposition could be more wide of the fact. Whatever
may have been the character of the men who legis-
lated for France afterward, no thoughtful student
of history can deny, despite all the arguments and
sneers of English Tory statesmen and historians,

---

* For striking pictures of this feeling among the younger
generation of Frenchmen, see Challamel, Sur la Révolution, p.
305. For general history of John Law's paper money, see
Henri Martin, Histoire de France; also Blanqui, Histoire de
l'Économie Politique, vol. ii, pp. 65–87; also Senior on Paper
Money, section iii, Part I; also Thiers.

that few more keen-sighted and patriotic legislative bodies have ever sat upon this earth than this first French Constituent Assembly. In it were such men as Sieyès, Bailly, Necker, Mirabeau, Talleyrand, Dupont, and a multitude of others who, in various sciences and in the political world, had already shown, and were destined afterward to show, themselves among the strongest and shrewdest men that Europe has yet seen.

But the current toward paper money had become irresistible. It was constantly urged, and with a great show of force, that if any nation could safely issue paper money, France was now that nation; that she was fully warned by her severe experience under John Law; that she was now a constitutional government, controlled by an enlightened, patriotic people; not as in the days of the former issue of paper money, an absolute monarchy controlled by politicians and adventurers; that she was able to secure every franc of her paper money by a virtual mortgage of a landed domain vastly greater in value than the entire issue; that, with men like Bailly, Mirabeau, and Necker, at her head, she could not commit the financial mistakes and crimes from which France had suffered when at the head stood John Law and the Regent and Cardinal Dubois.

Oratory prevailed over science and experience. In December, 1789, came the first decree. After much discussion it was decided to issue four hundred million francs in paper money, based upon the landed property of the nation as its security. The deliberations on this first decree, and on the bill carrying it into effect, were most interesting; prominent in the debate were Necker, Dupont, Maury, Cazalès, Bailly, and many others hardly inferior. The discussion was certainly very able; no person can read it at length in the Moniteur, or even in the summaries of the parliamentary history, without feeling that English historians have done wretched injustice to those men who were then endeavoring to stand between France and ruin.

At last, in April, 1790, the four hundred million francs were issued in *assignats*—paper money secured by a pledge of productive real estate, and bearing interest to the holder at three per cent. No irredeemable currency has ever claimed a more scientific and practical guarantee for its goodness and for its proper action on public finances. On one side it had what the world universally recognized as the most practical security—a mortgage on productive real estate of vastly greater value than the issue. On the other hand, as the notes bore interest, there was every reason for their being withdrawn from circulation whenever they became redundant.*

As speedily as possible the notes were put in circulation. Unlike those issued in John Law's time, they were engraved in the best style of the art. To stimulate loyalty, the portrait of the king was placed in the center; to stimulate patriotism, patriotic legends and emblems surrounded him; to stimulate public cupidity, the amount of interest which the note would yield each day to its holder was printed in the margin; and the whole was duly garnished with stamps and signatures, showing that it was under careful registration and control.† Having thus given France a new currency, the National Assembly, to explain its advantages, issued an address to the French people. In this address the Assembly spoke of the nation as "delivered by this grand means from all uncertainty, and from all ruinous results of the credit system." It foretold that this issue "would bring back into the public treasury, into commerce, and into all branch-

---

* See Buchez and Roux, Histoire Parlémentaire, vol. v, p. 321, *et seq.* For an argument to prove that the assignats were after all not so well secured as John Law's money, see Storch, Économie Politique, vol. iv, p. 160.

† For specimens of this issue, as of John Law's notes and of nearly every issue during the French Revolution, see the A. D. White collection as above.

2

es of industry, strength, abundance, and prosperity." *

Some of the arguments used in this address are worth recalling:

"Paper money is without inherent value, unless it represents some special property. Without representing some special property it is inadmissible in trade to compete with a metallic currency, which has a value real and independent of the public action; therefore it is that the paper money which has only the public authority as its basis has always caused ruin where it has been established; that is the reason why the bank notes of 1720, issued by John Law, after having caused terrible evils, have only left frightful memories. Therefore it is that the National Assembly has not wished to expose you to this danger, but has given this new paper money, not only a value derived from the national authority, but a value real and immutable; a value which permits it to sustain advantageously a competition with the precious metals themselves." †

But the final declaration is perhaps the most interesting. It was as follows:

" These assignats, bearing interest as they do,

---

* See Addresse de l'Assemblée Nationale sur les Émissions d'Assignats Monnaies, p. 5.

† Ibid., p. 10.

will soon be considered better than the coin now hoarded, and will again bring it out into circulation."

This legislation caused great joy. Among the various utterances of this feeling was the public letter of M. Sarot directed to the editor of the Journal of the National Assembly, and scattered throughout France. M. Sarot is hardly able to contain himself as he anticipates the prosperity and glory that this issue of paper is to bring to his country. One thing only vexes him, and that is the pamphlet of M. Bergasse against the assignats; therefore it is that after a long series of arguments and protestations, in order to give a final proof of his confidence in the paper money, and his entire skepticism as to the evils predicted by Bergasse and others, M. Sarot solemnly lays his house, garden, and furniture upon the altar of his country, and offers to sell them for paper money alone.*

The first result of this issue was apparently all that the most sanguine could desire; the treasury was at once greatly relieved; a portion of the public debt was paid; creditors were encouraged; credit revived; ordinary expenses were met, and the paper money having thus been passed from the

---

* See Lettre de M. Sarot, Paris, April 19, 1790.

Government into the midst of the people, trade was revived, and all difficulties seemed past. The anxieties of Necker, the prophecies of Bergasse, Maury, and Cazalès, seemed proven utterly futile. And, indeed, it is quite possible that, if the national authorities had stopped with this issue, few of the evils which afterward arose would have been severely felt; the four hundred millions of paper money then issued had simply taken the place of a similar amount of specie. But soon there came another result: times grew less easy; by the end of August, within four months after the issue of the four hundred million assignats, the Government had spent them, and was again in distress.* The old remedy immediately and naturally occurred to the minds of men. Thoughtless persons throughout the country began to cry out for another issue of paper; thoughtful men then began to recall what their fathers had told them about the seductive path of paper-money issues in John Law's time, and to remember the prophecies that they themselves had heard in the debate on the first issue of assignats less than six months before.

In that debate, as we have seen, Maury and Ca-

---

* Von Sybel, History of the French Revolution, vol. i, p. 252.

zalès foretold trouble. Necker, who was less sus-
pected of reactionary tendencies, had certainly
feared danger. The strong opponents of paper
had prophesied, at that time, that, once on the
downward path of inflation, the nation could not
be restrained, and that more issues would follow.
The supporters of the first issue had asserted that
this was a calumny; that France could and would
check these issues whenever she desired.

The condition of opinion in the Assembly was,
therefore, chaotic; a few schemers and dreamers
were loud and outspoken for paper money; many
of the more shallow and easy-going were inclined
to yield; the more thoughtful endeavored man-
fully to breast the current.

One man there was who had strength to stand
this pressure: Mirabeau. He was the popular
idol, the great orator of the Assembly; and he was
much more than a great orator: he had carried the
nation through some of its greatest dangers by a
boldness almost godlike; in the various conflicts he
had shown not only oratorical boldness, but a foresight of great value at the beginning of a revolution. As to his real opinion upon an irredeemable
currency, there can be no doubt. It was the opinion which all true statesmen have held, before his
time and since, in his own country, in England, in

America, in every modern civilized nation.   In his
letter to Cerutti, written in January, 1789, hardly
six months before, he spoke of paper money as "a
nursery of tyranny, corruption, and delusion; a
veritable debauch of authority in delirium."   In
his private letters written at this very time, which
were revealed at a later period, he showed that he
was fully aware of the dangers of inflation, but he
yielded to the pressure: partly because he thought
it important to relieve the treasury at once; partly
because he thought it important to sell the Government lands rapidly to the people, and so develop
speedily a large class of small landholders, pledged
to stand by the Government which gave them their
titles; partly, doubtless, from a love of immediate
rather than remote applause; and wholly in a vague
hope that the severe, inexorable laws of finance,
which had brought heavy punishments upon gov-
ernments emitting an irredeemable currency in
other lands, at other times, might, in some way,
be warded off from France, at this time.*

The question was brought up by Montesquiou's
report on the 27th of August.   This report, though
somewhat noncommittal, leaned, on the whole, to-

---

* For Mirabeau's real opinion on irredeemable paper, see
letter to Cerutti, in leading article of the Moniteur; also
Mémoires de Mirabeau, vol. vii, pp. 23, 24, and elsewhere.

ward an additional issue of paper. It goes on to declare that the original issue of four hundred millions, though opposed at the beginning, had proved successful; that assignats are the most economical method, though they have dangers; and as a climax came the declaration, "We must save the country." Still the committee hesitated to advise the new issue.*

Upon this report, on the 27th of August, 1790, Mirabeau made a striking speech. He confessed that he had at first feared the issue of assignats, but that he now dared urge it; that experience had shown the issue of paper money most serviceable; that the report proved the first issue of assignats a great success; that public affairs had come out of distress satisfactorily; that ruin had been averted, and credit established. He then argues that there is a difference between paper money of the old sort, from which the nation had suffered so much in John Law's time, and paper money of the new issue; he declares that the French nation is now enlightened, and says, "Deceptive subtleties can no longer deceive patriots and men of sense in this matter." He then goes on to say, "We must accomplish that which we have begun," and declared that

---

* See Moniteur, August 27, 1790.

there must be one more large issue of paper, guaranteed by the national lands and by the good faith of the French nation. To show how practical the system is, he insists that just as soon as paper money shall become too abundant it will be absorbed in rapid purchases of national lands; and a very striking comparison is made between this self-adjusting, self-converting system and the rains descending in showers upon the earth, then in swelling rivers discharged into the sea, then drawn up in vapor, and finally scattered over the earth again in rapidly fertilizing showers. He predicts that the members will be surprised at the astonishing success of this paper money, and that there will be none too much of it.*

His theory grows by what it feeds upon, as the paper-money theory has always done; toward the close, in a burst of eloquence, he suggests that assignats be created to an amount sufficient to cover the national debt, and that all the national lands be exposed for sale immediately, predicting that prosperity will thus return to the nation, and that all classes will find this additional issue of paper money a great blessing.

This speech was frequently interrupted by ap-

* Moniteur, August 28, 1790.

plause; by a unanimous vote it was ordered printed, and copies were spread throughout France. The impulse given by it can be seen throughout all the discussion afterward: Gouy arises and proposes to liquidate the debt of twenty-four hundred millions, to use his own words, " by one single operation— grand, simple, magnificent " : * This operation is the emission of twenty-four hundred millions in legal-tender notes, and a law that specie be not accepted in purchasing national lands. His demagogism blooms forth magnificently. He advocates an appeal to the people, who, to use his flattering expression, "ought alone to give the law in a matter so interesting." The newspapers of the period, in reporting his speech, note it with the very significant remark, " This discourse was loudly applauded."

To him replies Savarin. He calls attention to the depreciation of assignats already felt. He tries to make the Assembly see that natural laws work as certainly in France as elsewhere; and predicts that if this new issue be made there will come a depreciation of thirty per cent. He is followed by the Abbé Gouttes, who declares—what seems very

* " Par une seule opération, grande, simple, magnifique " (see Moniteur).

grotesque to those who have read the history of
an irredeemable paper currency in any country—
that new issues of paper money "will supply a circulating material which will protect public morals
from corruption." *

Into the midst of this debate is brought a report by Necker. Most earnestly he endeavors to
dissuade the Assembly from the proposed issue;
suggests that other means can be found for accom-
plishing the result, and predicts terrible evils. But
the current is again running too fast. The only
result is, that Necker is spurned as a man of the
past.† He at last sends in his resignation, and
leaves France forever. The paper-money demagogues shout for joy at his departure; their chorus
rings through the journalism of the time. No
words can express their contempt for a man who
can not see the advantages of filling the treasury
with the issues of a printing press. Marat, Hébert,
and Camille Desmoulins, are especially jubilant.‡

Continuing the debate, Rewbell attacks Necker,
saying that assignats are not at par because there is
not yet enough of them; he insists that payments

---

* Moniteur, August 29, 1790.

† See Lacretelle, 18ᵐᵉ Siècle, vol. viii, pp. 84–87; also Thiers
and Mignet.

‡ See Hatin, Histoire de la Presse en France, vols. v and vi.

for public lands be received in assignats alone; and
suggests that the church bells of the kingdom be
melted down into small money. Le Brun attacks
the whole scheme in the Assembly, as he had done
in the committee; declaring that the proposal, instead of relieving the nation, will wreck it. The
papers of the time very significantly say that at this
arose many murmurs. Chabroux comes to the
rescue. He says that the issue of assignats will relieve the distress of the people, and presents very
neatly the new theory of paper money and its basis
in the following words: "The earth is the source of
value; you can not distribute the earth in a circulating value, but this paper becomes representative
of that value, and it is evident that the creditors of
the nation will not be injured by taking it." On
the other hand, appeared in the leading paper, the
Moniteur, a very thoughtful article against paper
money, which sums up all by saying, "It is, then,
evident that all paper which can not at the will of
the bearer be converted into specie can not discharge
the functions of money." This article goes on to
cite Mirabeau's former opinion in his letter to
Cerutti, published in 1789; the famous opinion that
"paper money is a nursery of tyranny, corruption,
and delusions; a veritable orgy of authority in delirium." Lablache, in the Assembly, quotes the

saying that "paper money is the emetic of great states." *

Boutidoux follows in favor of paper money, and calls the assignats "*un papier terre*," or land converted into paper. Boisandry answers vigorously, and foretells evil results. Pamphlets continue to be issued, among them one so pungent that it is brought into the Assembly and read there. The truth which it brings out with great clearness is that doubling the quantity of money or substitutes for money in a nation simply increases prices, disturbs values, alarms capital, diminishes legitimate enterprise, and so decreases the demand both for products and for labor; that the only persons to be helped by it are the rich who have large debts to pay. This pamphlet was signed "A Friend of the People." It was received with great applause by the thoughtful part of the Assembly. Dupont, who had stood by Necker in the debate on the first issue of assignats, arises, avows the pamphlet to be his, and says sturdily that he has always voted against the emission of irredeemable paper and always will.

But far more important than any other argument against inflation was the speech of Talleyrand.

---

* See Moniteur, August 29, 1790.

He had been among the boldest and most radical French statesmen. He it was who, more than any other, had carried the extreme measure of taking into the possession of the nation the great landed estates of the Church. He now adopts a judicial tone—attempts to show to the Assembly the very simple truth that the effect of a second issue of assignats may be different from the first; that the first was evidently needed ; that the second may be as injurious as the first was useful. He exhibits various weak points in the inflation fallacies, and presents forcibly the trite truth that no laws and no decrees can keep large issues of irredeemable paper at a par with specie.

In his speech occur these words: " You can, indeed, arrange it so that the people shall be forced to take a thousand francs in paper for a thousand francs in specie; but you can never arrange it so that a man shall be obliged to give a thousand francs in specie for a thousand francs in paper. In that fact is imbedded the entire question ; and on account of that fact the whole system fails." *

The nation at large now began to take part in the debate ; thoughtful men saw that here was the

---

* See speech in Moniteur; also in Appendix to Thiers's History of the French Revolution.

turning point between good and evil; that the nation stood at the parting of the ways. Most of the great commercial cities bestirred themselves and sent up remonstrances against the new emission, twenty-five being opposed and seven in favor of it. But on September 27, 1790, came Mirabeau's great final speech. In this he dwelt first on the political necessity involved, declaring that the most pressing need was to get the Government lands into the hands of the people, and so to commit the class of landholders thus created to the nation, and against the old privileged classes.

Through the rest of the speech there is one leading point enforced with all his eloquence and ingenuity—the thorough excellence of the proposed currency and the stability of its security. He declares that, being based on the pledge of public lands, and convertible into them, the notes are better secured than if redeemable in specie; that the precious metals are only employed in the secondary arts, while the French paper money represents the first and most real of all property, the source of all production, the *land* itself; that, while other nations have been obliged to emit paper money, none has ever been so fortunate as the French nation, for none has ever before been able to give landed security for its paper; that whoever takes French paper money has practically a mortgage to secure it, on landed property which can be easily sold to satisfy his claims, while other nations have only been able to give a vague claim on the entire nation. " And," he cries, " I would rather have a mortgage on a garden than on a kingdom ! "

Other arguments of his are more demagogical. He declares that the only interests affected will be those of bankers and capitalists, but that manufacturers will see prosperity restored to them. Some of his arguments seem almost puerile, as when he says, " If gold has been hoarded through timidity or malignity, the issue of paper will show that gold is not necessary, and it will then come forth." But as a whole the speech was brilliant ; it was often interrupted by applause ; it settled the question. People did not stop to consider that it was the dashing speech of a bold orator, and not the matured judgment of an expert in finance ; they did not see that calling Mirabeau to decide upon a financial policy, because he had shown boldness in danger and strength in conflict, was like calling a successful blacksmith to mend a watch.

In vain did Maury show that, while the first issues of John Law's paper had brought apparent prosperity, those that followed brought certain misery ; in vain did he quote from a book published in John Law's time, showing that Law was at first considered a patriot and friend of humanity; in vain did he hold up to the Assembly one of Law's bills, and appeal to their memories of the wretchedness brought on France by them; nothing could resist the eloquence of Mirabeau. Barnave follows; says that "Law's paper was based upon the phantoms of the Mississippi; ours upon the solid basis of ecclesiastical lands," and proves that the assignats can not depreciate further. Prudhomme's newspaper pours contempt over gold as security for the currency, extols real estate as the only true basis, and is fervent in praise of the convertibility and self-adjusting features of the proposed scheme. In spite of all this plausibility and eloquence, a large minority stood firm to their earlier principles; but on the 29th of September, by a vote of 508 to 423, the deed was done; a bill was passed authorizing the issue of eight hundred millions of new assignats, but solemnly declaring that in no case should the entire amount put in circulation exceed twelve hundred millions. To make assurance doubly sure, it also provided that, as fast as the assignats were paid into the treasury for land, they should be burned; and thus a healthful contraction be constantly maintained.

Great were the plaudits of the nation at this relief. Rejoicings were heard on every side. Among

the multitudes of pamphlets expressing this joy
which have come down to us, the "Friend of the
Revolution" is the most interesting. It begins as
follows: "Citizens, the deed is done. The assignats
are the keystone of the arch. It has just been hap-
pily put in position. Now I can announce to you
that the Revolution is finished, and there only re-
main one or two important questions. All the rest
is but a matter of detail which can not deprive us
any longer of the pleasure of admiring in its entirety
this important work. The provinces and the commercial cities which were at first alarmed at the
proposal to issue so much paper money, now send
expressions of their thanks; specie is coming out to
be joined with paper money. Foreigners come to
us from all parts of Europe to seek their happiness
under laws which they admire; and soon France,
enriched by her new property and by the national
industry which is preparing for fruitfulness, will
demand still another creation of paper money."

To make these prophecies good, every means
was taken to keep up the credit of this second issue
of assignats. Among the multitudes of pamphlets
issued for this purpose was one by Royer; it appeared September 14, 1790, and was entitled Re-
flections of a Patriotic Citizen upon the Emission
of Assignats. In this Royer gives many excellent

reasons why the assignats can not be depressed; and speaks of the argument against them as "vile clamors of people bribed to affect public opinion." He says to the National Assembly, "If it is necessary to create five thousand millions and more of this paper, decree such a creation gladly." He, too, predicts, as Mirabeau and others had done, the time when gold will lose all its value, since all exchanges will be made with this admirably guaranteed paper, and therefore that coin will come out from the places where it is hoarded. He foretells prosperous times to France in case these great issues of paper are continued, and declares this "the only means to insure happiness, glory, and liberty, to the French nation."

France was now fully committed to a policy of inflation; and, if there had been any doubt of this before, it was soon proved by an act of the Government, very plausible, but none the less significant, as showing the exceeding difficulty of stopping a nation once in the full tide of a depreciated currency. The old cry of the "lack of a circulating medium" broke forth again; and especially loud were the clamors for more small bills. This resulted in an evasion of the solemn pledge that the circulation should not go above twelve hundred millions, and that all assignats returned to the treasury for land should immediately be burned. Within a short time there had been received into the treasury for lands one hundred and sixty million francs in paper. By the terms of the previous acts this amount ought to have been retired. Instead of this, under the plea of necessity, one hundred millions were reissued in the form of small notes.*

Yet this was but as a drop of cold water to a parched throat. Although there was already a rise in prices which showed that the amount needed for circulation had been exceeded, the cry for "more circulating medium" was continued. The pressure for new issues became stronger and stronger. The Parisian populace and the Jacobin Club were especially loud in their demands for them; and a few months later, on June 19, 1791, with few speeches, in a silence very ominous, a new issue was made of six hundred millions more; less than nine months after the former great issue, with its solemn pledges as to keeping down the amount in circulation. With the exception of a few thoughtful men, the whole nation again sang pæans.

In this comparative ease of a new issue is seen the action of a law in finance as certain as the action

---

* See Von Sybel, History of the Revolution, vol. i, p. 265.

of a similar law in natural philosophy. If a material body fall from a height, its velocity is accel-
erated, by a well-known law in physics, in a constantly increasing ratio : so in issues of irredeemable
currency, in obedience to the theories of a legislative body, or of the people at large, there is a natural law of rapidly increasing issue and depreciation.
The first inflation bill was passed with great difficulty, after a very sturdy resistance, and by a majority of a few score out of nearly a thousand
votes; but you observe now that new inflation
measures are passed more and more easily, and you
will have occasion to see the working of this same
law in a more striking degree as this history develops itself.

Nearly all Frenchmen now became desperate
optimists, declaring that inflation is prosperity.
Throughout France there came temporary good
feeling. The nation was becoming fairly inebriated
with paper money. The good feeling was that of a
drunkard after his draught; and it is to be noted, as
a simple historical fact, corresponding to a physio-
logical fact, that, as the draughts of paper money
came faster, the periods of succeeding good feeling
grew shorter.

Various bad signs had begun to appear. Immediately after this last issue came a depreciation of

from eight to ten per cent; but it is very curious to note the general reluctance to assign the right reason. The decline in the purchasing power of paper money was in obedience to one of the simplest laws in social physics; but France had now gone beyond her thoughtful statesmen, and took refuge in unwavering optimism; giving any explanation of the new difficulties rather than the right one. A leading member of the Assembly insisted, in an elaborate speech, that the cause of depreciation was simply want of knowledge and of confidence among the rural population, and proposed means of enlightening them. La Rochefoucauld proposed to issue an address to the people, showing the goodness of the currency and the absurdity of preferring coin. The address was unanimously voted. As well might they have attempted to show that, if, from the liquid made up by mixing a quart of wine and two quarts of water, a gill be taken, this gill will possess all the exhilarating value of the original, undiluted beverage.

Attention was next aroused by another menacing fact—specie was fast disappearing. The explanations for this fact also displayed wonderful ingenuity in finding false reasons and evading the true one. A very common explanation may be found in Prud-

homme's newspaper, Les Révolutions de Paris, of
January 17, 1791, which declared that "coin will
keep rising until the people have hung a broker." *
Another popular theory was that the Bourbon fam-
ily were in some miraculous way drawing off all
solid money to the chief centers of their intrigues
in Germany.†

Still another favorite idea was that English emissaries were in the midst of the people, instilling no-
tions hostile to paper.   Great efforts were made to
find these emissaries, and more than one innocent
person experienced the popular wrath, under the
supposition that he was engaged in raising gold and
depressing paper.‡   Even Talleyrand, shrewd as he
was, insisted that the cause was simply that the im-
ports were too great and the exports too little.#   As
well might he explain the fact that, when oil is mingled with water, water sinks to the bottom, by saying that it is because the oil rises to the top.   This
disappearance of specie was the result of a natural
law as simple and sure in its action as gravitation:
the superior currency had been withdrawn because

---

* See also De Goncourt, Société Française, for other explanations.

† See Les Révolutions de Paris, vol. ii. p. 216.

‡ See Challamel, Les Français sous la Révolution; also
Senior, On Some Effects of Paper Money, p. 82.

See Buchez and Roux, vol. x, p. 216.

an inferior could be used.* Some efforts were made to remedy this. In the municipality of Quillebœuf the sum of 817 marks in specie having been found in the possession of a citizen, the money was seized and sent to the Assembly. The good people of that town treated this hoarded gold as the result of some singularly unpatriotic wickedness or madness, instead of seeing that it was but the sure result of a law, working in every land and time, when certain causes are present. Marat followed out this theory by asserting that death was the proper penalty for persons who thus hid their money. In order to supply the specie required a great number of church bells were melted down; but this also proved inadequate.

Still another troublesome fact began now to appear. Though paper money had increased in amount, prosperity had steadily diminished. In spite of all the paper issues business activity grew more and more spasmodic. Enterprise was chilled, and stagnation had set in. Mirabeau, in his speech which decided the second great issue of paper, had insisted that, though bankers might suffer, this issue would be of great service to manufacturers and re-

---

* For an admirable statement and illustration of the general action of this law, see Sumner, History of American Currency, pp. 157, 158; also Jevons, on Money, p. 80.

store their prosperity. The manufacturers were for a time deluded, but were at last rudely awakened from their delusions. The plenty of currency had at first stimulated production and created a great activity in manufactures, but soon the markets were glutted, and the demand was vastly diminished. In spite of the wretched financial policy of years gone by, and especially in spite of the Edict of Nantes, by which religious bigotry had driven out of the kingdom thousands of its most skillful workmen, the manufactures of France had before the Revolution come into full bloom. In the finer woolen and cotton goods, in silk and satin fabrics of all sorts, in choice pottery and porcelain, in manufactures of iron, steel, and copper, they had again taken their old place upon the Continent. All the previous changes had, at the worst, done no more than to inflict a momentary check on this highly developed system of manufactures; but what the bigotry of Louis XIV and the shiftlessness of Louis XV could not do in nearly a century was accomplished by this tampering with the currency in a few months. One manufactory after another stopped. At one town, Lodève, five thousand workmen were discharged from the cloth manufactories. Every cause except the right one was assigned for this. Heavy duties were put upon foreign goods. Everything that tar-

iffs and customhouses could do was done. Still the
great manufactories of Normandy were closed, those
of the rest of the kingdom speedily followed, and
vast numbers of workmen in all parts of the country
were thrown out of employment.* Nor was this
the case alone in regard to home demand. The foreign demand, which had been at first stimulated,
soon fell off. In no way can this be better stated
than by one of the most thoughtful historians of
modern times : " It is true that at first the assignats
gave the same impulse to business in the city as in
the country, but the apparent improvement had no
firm foundation even in the towns. Whenever a
great quantity of paper money is suddenly issued
we invariably see a rapid increase of trade. The
great quantity of the circulating medium sets in
motion all the energies of commerce and manufactures ; capital for investment is more easily found
than usual, and trade perpetually receives fresh
nutriment. If this paper represents real credit,
founded upon order and legal security, from which
it can derive a firm and lasting value, such a movement may be the starting point of a great and widely
extended prosperity, as, for instance, the most splen-
did improvements in English agriculture were un-

---

* See De Goncourt, Société Française, p. 214.

doubtedly owing to the emancipation of the country bankers. If, on the contrary, the new paper is of precarious value, as was clearly seen to be the case with the French assignats as early as February, 1791, it can have no lasting, beneficial fruits. For the moment, perhaps, business receives an impulse, all the more violent because every one endeavors to invest his doubtful paper in buildings, machines, and goods, which under all circumstances retain some intrinsic value. Such a movement was witnessed in France in 1791, and from every quarter there came satisfactory reports of the activity of manufactures.

" But, for the moment, the French manufacturers derived great advantage from this state of things. As their products could be so cheaply paid for, orders poured in from foreign countries to such a degree that it was often difficult for the manufacturers to satisfy their customers. It is easy to see that prosperity of this kind must very soon find its limit. . . . When a further fall in the assignats took place it would necessarily collapse at once, and be succeeded by a crisis all the more destructive the more deeply men had engaged in speculation under the influence of the first favorable prospects." *

---

* See Von Sybel, History of the French Revolution, vol. i, pp. 281, 283.

Thus came a collapse in manufacturing and commerce, just as it had come before in France; just as it came afterward in Austria, Russia, America, and in all other countries where men have tried to build up prosperity on irredeemable paper.*

All this breaking down of the manufactures and commerce of the nation made fearful inroads on the greater fortunes; but upon the lesser fortunes, and the little accumulated properties of the masses of the nation who relied upon their labor, it pressed with intense severity.

Still another difficulty appeared. There had come a complete uncertainty as to the future. In the spring of 1791 no one knew whether a piece of paper money representing a hundred francs would, a month later, have a purchasing power of a hundred francs, or ninety francs, or eighty, or sixty. The result was that capitalists feared to embark their means in business. Enterprise received a mortal blow. Demand for labor was still further dimin-

---

* For proofs that issues of irredeemable paper at first stimulated manufactures and commerce in Austria, and afterward ruined them, see Storch's Économie Politique, vol. iv, p. 223, note; and for the same effect produced by the same causes in Russia, see ibid., end of vol. iv. For the same effects in America, see Sumner's History of American Currency. For general statement of effect of inconvertible issues on foreign exchanges, see McLeod on Banking, p. 186.

ished; and here came an additional cause of misery. By this uncertainty all far-reaching undertakings were killed. The business of France dwindled into a mere living from hand to mouth. This state of things, too, while it bore heavily against the interests of the moneyed classes, was still more ruinous to those in more moderate and, most of all, to those in straitened circumstances. With the masses of the people, the purchase of every article of supply became a speculation—a speculation in which the professional speculator had an immense advantage over the ordinary buyer. Says the most brilliant of apologists for French revolutionary statesmanship, " Commerce was dead; betting took its place."*

Nor was there any compensating advantage to the mercantile classes. The merchant was forced to add to his ordinary profit a sum sufficient to cover probable or possible fluctuations in value. And while prices of products thus went higher, the wages of labor, owing to the number of workmen who were thrown out of employ, went lower.

But these evils, though very great, were small compared to those far more deep-seated signs of disease which now showed themselves throughout

* See Louis Blanc, Histoire de la Révolution Française, tome xii, p. 113.

the country. The first of these was the *obliteration of thrift* in the minds of the French people. The French are naturally a thrifty people; but, with such masses of money and with such uncertainty as to its future value, the ordinary motives for saving and care diminished, and a ·loose luxury spread throughout the country. A still worse outgrowth of this feeling was the increase of speculation and gambling. With the plethora of paper currency in 1791 appeared the first evidences of that cancerous disease which always follows large issues of irredeemable currency—a disease more permanently injurious to a nation than war, pestilence, or famine. At the great metropolitan centers grew a luxurious, speculative, stock-gambling body, which, like a malignant tumor, absorbed into itself the strength of the nation, and sent out its cancerous fibers to the remotest hamlets. At these city centers abundant wealth was piled up. In the country at large there grew dislike of steady labor and contempt for moderate gains and simple living. In a pamphlet published May, 1791, we see how, in regard to this also, public opinion was blinded. The author calls attention to the frightful increase of gambling in values of all sorts in these words: "What shall I say of the stockjobbing, as frightful as it is scandalous, which goes on in Paris under the very eyes of our legislators, a most terrible evil, yet under the present circumstances a necessary evil?" The author also speaks of these stock gamblers as using the most insidious means to influence public opinion in favor of their measures; and then proposes, seriously, a change in various matters of detail, thinking that this would prove a sufficient remedy for an evil which had its roots far down in the whole system of irredeemable currency.* As well might a physician prescribe a pimple wash for a diseased liver.

Now began to be seen more plainly some of the many ways in which an inflation policy robs the working classes. As these knots of plotting schemers at the city centers were becoming bloated with sudden wealth, the producing classes of the country, though having in their possession more and more currency, grew lean. In the schemes and speculations put forth by stockjobbers, and stimulated by the printing of more currency, multitudes of small fortunes throughout the country were absorbed, and, while these many small fortunes were lost, a few swollen fortunes were rapidly aggregated in the city centers. This crippled a large class in the country districts, which had employed a great num-

---

* See Extrait du Registre des Delibérations de la Section de la Bibliothèque, May 3, 1791, pp. 4, 5.

ber of workmen ; and created a small class, in the cities, which employed a great number of lackeys.

In the cities now arose a luxury and license which is a greater evil even than the plundering which ministers to it. In the country the gambling spirit spread more and more. Says the same thoughtful historian whom I have already quoted : " What a prospect for a country when its rural population was changed into a great band of gamblers ! " *

Nor was this reckless and corrupt spirit confined to business men ; it began to break out in official circles, and public men who, a few years before, had been pure in motive and above all probability of taint, became luxurious, reckless, cynical, and finally corrupt. Mirabeau himself, who, not many months before, had risked imprisonment and even death to establish constitutional government, was now—at this very time—secretly receiving heavy bribes : when at the downfall of the monarchy, a few years later, the famous iron chest of the Tuileries was opened, there were found evidences that, in this carnival of inflation and corruption, Mirabeau himself had been a regularly paid servant of the court.†

---

* Von Sybel, vol. i, p. 273.

† For general account, see Thiers's Revolution, chapter xiv ; also Lacretelle, vol. viii, p. 109 ; also Memoirs of Mallet Du Pan. For a good account of the intrigues between the court and

The artful plundering of the people at large was bad enough, but worse still was this growing corruption in official and legislative circles. Out of the speculating and gambling of the inflation period grew luxury, and out of this grew corruption. It grew as naturally as a fungus on a muck heap. It was first felt in business operations, but soon began to be seen in the legislative body and in journalism. Mirabeau was by no means the only example. Such members of the legislative body as Jullien, of Toulouse, Delaunay, of Angers, Fabre d'Eglantine, and their disciples, were among the most noxious of those conspiring by legislative action to raise and depress securities for stockjobbing purposes. Bribery of legislators followed as a matter of course. Delaunay, Jullien, and Chabot, accepted a bribe of five hundred thousand francs for aiding legislation calculated to promote the purposes of certain stockjobbers. It is some comfort to know that nearly all concerned lost their heads for it.*

Mirabeau, and of the prices paid him, see Reeve, Democracy and Monarchy in France, vol. i, pp. 213-220. For a very striking caricature published after the iron chest in the Tuileries was opened, and the evidence of bribery of Mirabeau revealed, see Challamel, Musée de la Révolution Française, vol. i, p. 341. Mirabeau is represented as a skeleton sitting on a pile of letters, holding the French crown in one hand and a purse of gold in the other.

* Thiers, chapter ix.

It is true that the number of these corrupt legislators was small, far less than alarmists led the nation to suppose, but there were enough to cause widespread distrust, cynicism, and want of faith in any patriotism or any virtue.

Even worse than this was the breaking down of morals in the country at large, resulting from the sudden building up of ostentatious wealth in a few large cities, and the gambling, speculative spirit fostered in the small towns and rural districts.

Yet even a more openly disgraceful result of this paper money was to come, and this was the decay of any true sense of national honor or good faith. The patriotism which the fear of the absolute monarchy, the machinations of a court party, the menaces of the army, and the threats of all monarchical Europe, had been unable to shake, was gradually disintegrated by this same stockjobbing, speculative habit fostered by the new currency. At the outset, in the discussions preliminary to the first issue of paper money, Mirabeau and others who had favored it had insisted that patriotism, as well as an enlightened self-interest, would lead the people to keep up the value of paper money. The very opposite of this was now found to be the case. There now appeared, as another outgrowth of this disease, what has always been seen under similar

4

circumstances. It is a result of previous evils and a cause of future evils. This outgrowth was the creation of a great debtor class in the nation, directly interested in the depreciation of the currency in which their debts were to be paid. The nucleus of this debtor class was formed by those who had purchased the church lands from the Government. Only small payments down had been required, and the remainder was to be paid in small installments spread over much time: an indebtedness had thus been created, by a large number of people, to the amount of hundreds of millions. This large body of debtors, of course, soon saw that their interest was to depreciate the currency in which their debts were to be paid; and soon they were joined by a far more influential class; by that class whose speculative tendencies had been stimulated by the abundance of paper money, and who had gone largely into debt, looking for a rise in nominal values. Soon demagogues of the viler sort in the political clubs began to pander to this debtor class; soon important members of this debtor class were to be found intriguing in the Assembly—often on the seats of the Assembly and in places of public trust. Before long, the debtor class became a powerful body, extending through all ranks of society. From the stock gambler who sat in the Assembly to the small land speculator in the rural districts; from the sleek inventor of *canards* on the Paris Exchange to the lying stockjobber in the market town, all pressed vigorously for new issues of paper; all were able, apparently, to demonstrate to the people that in new issues of paper lay the only chance for national prosperity.

This great debtor class, relying on the multitude who could be approached by superficial arguments, soon gained control. Strange as it may seem, to those who have not watched the same causes at work at a previous period in France, and at various periods in other countries, while every issue of paper money really made matters worse, a superstition steadily gained ground among the people at large that, if only *enough* paper money were issued and more cunningly handled, the poor would be made rich. Henceforth all opposition was futile. In December, 1791, a report was made in the Assembly in favor of a fourth great issue of three hundred millions more of paper money. In regard to this report, Chambon says that more money is needed, but asks, "Will you, in a moment when stockjobbing is carried on with such fury, give it new power by adding so much more money to the circulation?" But such high considerations were now little regarded. Dorisy declares that " there is not enough money yet in circulation; that, if there were more, the sales of national lands would be more rapid." And the official report of his speech declares that these words were applauded.

Dorisy declares that the Government lands are worth at least thirty-five hundred million francs, and asks: "Why should members ascend the tribune and disquiet France? Fear nothing; your currency reposes upon a sound mortgage." Then follows a glorification of the patriotism of the French people, which, he asserts, will carry the nation through all its difficulties.

Becquet follows, declaring that the "circulation is becoming more rare every day."

On December 17, 1791, a new issue was ordered of three hundred millions more, making in all twenty-one hundred millions authorized. Coupled with this was the declaration that the total amount of circulation should never reach more than sixteen hundred millions. What such limitations were worth may be judged from the fact that not only had the declaration made hardly a year before, limiting the amount in circulation to twelve hundred millions, been violated, but the declaration, made hardly a *month* before, in which the Assembly had as solemnly limited the amount of circulation to fourteen hundred millions, had also been

repudiated. The evils which we have already seen
arising from the earlier issues were now aggravated.

But the most curious thing evolved out of all
this chaos was a *new system of political economy.*
In the speeches about this time, we begin to find it
declared that, after all, a depreciated currency is a
blessing; that gold and silver form an unsatisfac-
tory standard for measuring values; that it is a
good thing to have a currency that will not go out
of the kingdom, and which separates France from
other nations; that thus shall manufactures be encouraged; that commerce with other nations is a
curse, and every hindrance to it a blessing; that
the laws of political economy, however applicable
in other times, are not applicable to this particular
time, and, however operative in other nations, are
not operative in France; that the ordinary rules of
political economy are perhaps suited to the minions
of despotism, but not to the free and enlightened
inhabitants of France at the close of the eighteenth
century; that the whole present state of things, so
far from being an evil, is a blessing. All these
ideas, and others quite as striking, are brought to the
surface in the debates on the various new issues.*

---

* See especially Discours de Fabre d'Eglantine, in Moniteur
for August 11, 1793; also debate in Moniteur of September 15,
1793; also Prudhomme's Révolutions de Paris.

Within four months comes another report to the Assembly as ingenious as those preceding. It declares: "Your committee are thoroughly persuaded that the amount of circulating medium before the Revolution was greater than that of the assignats to-day; but then the money circulated slowly, and now it passes rapidly, so that one thousand million assignats do the work of two thousand millions of specie." The report foretells further increase in prices, but by some curious jugglery reaches a conclusion favorable to further inflation.

The result was that on April 30, 1792, came the fifth great issue of paper money, amounting to three hundred millions; and at about the same time Cambon sneered ominously at public creditors as "rich people, old financiers, and bankers." Soon payment was suspended on dues to public creditors for all amounts exceeding ten thousand francs.

This was hailed by many as a measure in the interests of the poorer classes of people, but the result was that it injured them most of all. Henceforward, until the end of this history, capital was taken from labor and locked up in all the ways that financial ingenuity could devise. All that saved thousands of laborers in France from starvation was that they were drafted off into the army and sent to be killed on foreign battlefields.

In February, 1792, assignats were over thirty per cent below par.*

On the last day of July, 1792, came another brilliant report from Fouquet, showing that the total amount already issued was about twenty-four hundred millions, but claiming that the national lands were worth a little more than this sum. Though it was easy for any shrewd mind to find out the fallacy of this, a decree was passed issuing three hundred millions more. By this the prices of everything were again enhanced save one thing, and that one thing was *labor*. Strange as it may at first appear, while all products had been raised enormously in price by the depreciation of the currency, the stoppage of so many manufactories, and the withdrawal of capital, caused wages in the summer of 1792, after all the inflation, to be as small as they had been four years before—namely, fifteen sous per day.† No more striking example can be seen of the truth uttered by Daniel Webster, that " of all the contrivances for cheating the laboring class of mankind, none has been more effectual than that which deludes them with paper money."

Issue after issue followed at intervals of a few

---

* Von Sybel, vol. i, pp. 509, 510.

† See Von Sybel, vol. i, p. 515; also Villeneuve Bargemont, Histoire de l'Économie Politique, vol. ii, p. 213.

months until on December 14, 1792, we have an
official statement to the effect that thirty-four hundred millions had been put forth, of which six hundred millions had been burned, leaving in circulation twenty-eight hundred millions. When it is
remembered that there was little business to do,
and that the purchasing power of the *franc*, when
judged by the staple products of the country, was
about equal to half the present purchasing power of
our own dollar, it will be seen into what evils
France had drifted.* As this mania for paper ran
its course,. even the sous, obtained by melting down
the church bells, appear to have been driven out of
circulation; parchment money from twenty sous to
five was issued, and at last bills of one sou, and even
of half a sou, were put in circulation.†

But now another source of wealth opens to the
nation. There comes a confiscation of the large
estates of nobles and landed proprietors who had
fled the country. An estimate in 1793 makes the
value of these estates three billion francs. As a

---

* As to purchasing power of money at that time, see Arthur
Young, Travels in France during the Years 1787, 1788, and
1789.

† For notices of this small currency, with examples of sa-
tirical verses written upon it, see Challamel, Les Français sous
la Révolution," pp. 307, 308. See also Mercier, Le Nouveau
Paris, edition of 1800, chapter ccv, entitled Parchemin Monnoie.

consequence, the issues of paper money were continued in increased amounts, on the old theory that they were guaranteed by the solemn pledge of these lands belonging to the state. Early in 1793 the consequences of these overissues began to be more painfully evident to the people at large. Articles of common consumption became enormously dear, and the price was constantly rising. Orators in the clubs, local meetings, and elsewhere, endeavored to enlighten people by assigning every reason save the true one. They declaimed against the corruption of the ministry, the want of patriotism among the moderates, the intrigues of the emigrant nobles, the hard-heartedness of the rich, the monopolizing spirit of the merchants, the perversity of the shop keepers, and named these as causes of the difficulty.*

The washerwomen of Paris, finding soap so dear that they could scarcely purchase it, insisted that all the merchants who were endeavoring to save something of their little property by refusing to sell their goods for the worthless currency with which France was flooded, should be punished with death; the women of the markets, and the hangers-on of the Jacobin Club, called loudly for a law "to

---

* For Chaumette's brilliant argument to this effect, see Thiers, Shoberl's translation, published by Bentley, vol. iii, p. 248.

equalize the value of paper money and silver coin."
It was also demanded that a tax be laid especially
on the rich, to the amount of four hundred million
francs, to buy bread; and the National Convention,
which had now become the legislative body of the
French Republic, ordered that such a tax be levied.
Marat declared loudly that the people, by hanging
a few shopkeepers and plundering their stores,
could easily remove the trouble. The result was,
that on the 28th of February, 1793, at eight o'clock
in the evening, a mob of men and women in dis-
guise began plundering the stores and shops of
Paris. At first they demanded only bread; soon
they insisted on coffee and rice and sugar; at last
they seized everything on which they could lay
their hands—cloth, clothing, groceries, and luxuries
of every kind. Two hundred shops and stores
were plundered. This was endured for six hours,
and finally order was restored only by a grant of
seven million francs to buy off the mob. The new
political economy was beginning to bear its fruits.
One of its minor growths appeared at the City Hall
of Paris, where, in response to the complaints of
the plundered merchants, Roux declared, in the
midst of great applause, that "the shopkeepers
were only giving back to the people what they had
hitherto robbed them of."

This mob was thus bought off, but now came the most monstrous of all financial outgrowths of paper money, and yet it was an outgrowth perfectly logical. *Maximum* laws were passed—laws making the sales of goods compulsory, and fixing their price in paper money. As Von Sybel declares, " it was the most comprehensive attack on the rights of property, as far as our historical knowledge reaches, which was ever made in western Europe—an attack made in the heart of a great and civilized nation, and one which was not confined to the brains of a few idle dreamers, but practically carried out in all its terrible consequences. It was made with fiery fanaticism and unbridled passion, and yet with systematic calculation. Its originators—victorious at home and abroad—were perfectly free in their deliberations, and did not adopt their measures under the pressure of necessity or despair, but from deliberate choice. These are facts of universal significance, on which we ought to fix our attention all the more earnestly, because they have been disregarded, although they are fraught with the most important consequences." *

* See Von Sybel, vol. iii, pp. 11, 12. For general statements of theories underlying the *maximum*, see Thiers. For a very interesting picture, by an eyewitness, of the absurdities and miseries it caused, see Mercier, Nouveau Paris, edition of 1800,

I have said that these maximum laws were perfectly logical; they were so.   Whenever any nation intrusts to its legislators the issue of a currency not based on the idea of redemption in coin, it intrusts to them the power to raise or depress the value of every article in the possession of every citizen. Louis XIV claimed that all property in France was his own, and that what private persons held was as much his as if it were in his coffers.*   But even this falls short of the reality of the confiscating power exercised in a country where, instead of leaving values to be measured by a standard common to the whole world, they are left to be depressed or raised at the whim, caprice, or interest of a body of legislators.†   When this power is given, the power of fixing prices is naturally included in it, as the less is included in the greater.

chapter xliv. For summary of the Report of the Committee, with list of articles embraced under it, and for various interesting details, see Villeneuve Bargemont. Histoire de l'Économie Politique, vol. ii, pp. 213–239. For curious examples of severe penalties for very slight infringements of the law on the subject, see Louis Blanc, Histoire de la Révolution Française, tome x, p. 144.

* See Memoirs of Louis XIV for the Instruction of the Dauphin.

† For a simple exposition of the way in which the exercise of this power became simply confiscation of all private property in France, see Mallet Du Pan's Memoirs, London, 1852, vol. ii, p. 14.

The first result of the *maximum* was that every means was taken to evade the fixed price imposed; the farmers brought in as little produce as they possibly could. This caused scarcity, and the people of the large cities were put on an allowance.

Tickets were issued authorizing the bearer to obtain at the maximum prices a certain amount of bread, or sugar, or soap, or wood, or coal, to cover immediate necessities. *

It may be said that these measures were the result of the war then going on. Nothing could be more baseless than such an objection. The war was generally successful. It was pushed mainly upon foreign soil. Numerous contributions were levied upon the subjugated countries to support the French armies. The war was one of those of which the loss, falling apparently upon future generations, stimulates, in a sad way, trade and production in the generation in being. The main cause of these evils was the old false system of confiscating the property of an entire nation; keeping all values in fluctuation; discouraging all enterprise; paralyzing all energy; undermining sober habits; obliterating thrift; promoting extravagance and wild riot, by the issue of an irredeemable currency.

---

* See specimens of these tickets in A. D. W. Collection.

It has also been argued that the assignats sank
in value because they were not well secured—that
securing them on Government real estate was as
futile as if the United States were to secure notes
on its real estate in distant Territories. This objection is utterly fallacious. The Government lands
of our own country are remote from the centers of
capital, and difficult to examine: the French national real estate was near those centers—even in
them—and easy to examine. Our national real
estate is unimproved and unproductive: theirs was
improved and productive; the average productive-
ness of that in market was quite five per cent, in
ordinary times.*

It has also been objected that the attempt to
secure the assignats on Government real estate
failed because of the general want of confidence in
the title derived by the purchasers from the new
Government. Every thorough student of that
period must know that this is a misleading statement. Everything shows that the French people
generally had the most unwavering confidence in
the stability of the new Government during the

---

* Louis Blanc calls attention to this very fact in showing
the superiority of the French assignats to our Continental currency. See Louis Blanc, Histoire de la Révolution Française,
tome xii, p. 98.

greater part of the Revolution.   There were disbelievers in the perpetuity of it, just as there were
disbelievers in the perpetuity of the United States
throughout our recent civil war; but they were a
small minority.   Even granting that there was a
doubt as to investment in French lands, the French
people had certainly as much confidence in the secure possession of Government lands as any people
can ever have in large issues of Government bonds;
indeed, it is certain that they had far more confidence in their lands as a security than any modern
nation can have in large issues of convertible bonds
obtained by payments of irredeemable paper.   The
simple fact, as stated by John Stuart Mill, which
made assignats convertible into real estate unsuc-
cessful was that the vast majority of people could
not afford to make investments outside their business; and this fact is just as fatal to any attempt
to contract large issues of irredeemable paper by
making such issues convertible into bonds bearing low interest—save, perhaps, a bold, statesmanlike attempt, which seizes the best time and presses
every advantage, eschewing all "interconvertibility"
devices, and sacrificing everything to regain a sound
currency based on standards common to the entire
financial world.

On April 11, 1793, a law was passed to meet the

case of those who bought specie with paper. Nothing could be more natural than such purchases. Husbands who wished to make provision for their wives, fathers who wished to make provision for their children, desired to accumulate something of acknowledged value, and enormous prices in paper were paid for gold. The new law forbade the sale or exchange of specie for more than its nominal value in paper, with a penalty of six years' imprisonment in irons.*

It will doubtless astonish many to learn that, in spite of these evident results of too much currency, the old cry of a "scarcity of circulating medium" was not stilled; it appeared not long after each issue, no matter how large, and reappeared now.

But every thoughtful student of financial history knows that this cry always comes after such issues—nay, that it *must* come—because in obedience to a natural law there *is* a scarcity, or rather *insufficiency*, of currency just as soon as prices become adjusted to the new volume, and there comes some little revival of business with the usual increase of credit.

The cry of "insufficient amount of circulating

---

* See Von Sybel, vol. iii, p. 26; also Montgaillard, Histoire de la Révolution Française, p. 196.

medium " was again raised. The needs of the Government were pressing, and within a month after the passage of the fearful penal laws made necessary by the old issues, twelve-hundred millions more were sent forth.*

About ten days after this a law was passed making a forced loan of one thousand millions from the rich.† In August, 1793, appears a report by Cambon. No one can read it without being struck by its perverted ability.

But while Cambon's plan of dealing with the public debt has outlasted all revolutions since, his plan of dealing with the inflated currency came to speedy and wretched failure.

Very carefully he had devised a funding scheme which, taken in connection with his system of issues, was in effect what in these days would be called an " *interconvertibility scheme.*" By various degrees of persuasion or force holders of assignats were urged to convert them into evidences of national debt, bearing interest at five per cent,‡ with the understanding that if more paper were afterward

---

* For an excellent statement of the action of this law in our own country, see Sumner, p. 220.

† For a specimen of a Forced Loan Certificate, see A. D. W. Collection.

‡ See Cambon's Report, August 15, 1753, pp. 49–60; also Decree of August 15–24, 1793, § 31, chapters xcvi–ciii.

needed more would be issued. All in vain. The
official tables of depreciation show that the assignats
continued to fall; soon a forced loan calling in a
billion of these checked this fall, but only for a moment.* The "interconvertibility scheme" between
currency and bonds failed as dismally as the "interconvertibility scheme" between currency and land
had failed.

Soon after came a law confiscating the property
of all Frenchmen who left France before July 14,
1789, and who had not returned. This gave new
land to be mortgaged for the security of paper
money.

Month after month, year after year, new issues
went on. Meanwhile everything possible was done
to keep up the value of paper. In obedience to
those who believed with the market women of Paris,
as stated in their famous petition, that "laws should
be passed making paper as good as gold," Couthon,
on August 1, 1793, proposed and carried a law pun-
ishing any person who should sell assignats at less
than their nominal value, with imprisonment for
twenty years in chains. Two years later Couthon
carried a law making investments in foreign coun-

---

* See Tableau de Dépréciation du Papier Monnaie dans le
Département de la Seine.

tries by Frenchmen punishable with death; and to make this series of measures complete, to keep up paper at all hazards, on August 15, 1793, the national debt was virtually repudiated.*

But to the surprise of the great majority of the people in France, after the momentary spasm of fear had passed, the value of the assignats was found not to have been increased by these measures; on the contrary, they persisted in obeying the natural laws of finance, and as new issues increased their value decreased in a constant ratio. Nor did the most lavish aid of Nature avail to help matters. The paper money of the nation seemed to possess a magic power to transmute prosperity into adversity. The year 1794 was exceptionally fruitful; crops were abundant; and yet with the autumn came scarcity of provisions, and with the winter came famine. The reason is perfectly simple. The sequences in that whole history are absolutely logical. First, the Legislature had inflated the currency and raised prices enormously. Next, it had been forced to establish an arbitrary maximum price for produce. But this price, large as it seemed, was not equal to the real value of produce; many of the farmers, therefore, raised less produce or refrained from

---

* See Von Sybel, vol. iii, p. 172.

bringing what they had to market.* But, as is usual in such cases, the trouble was ascribed to everything rather than the real cause, and the most severe measures were established in all parts of the country to force farmers to bring produce to market, the millers to grind it, and the shopkeepers to sell it.† The issues of paper money continued. Toward the end of 1794 seven thousand million assignats were in circulation.‡ By the end of May, 1795, the circulation was increased to ten thousand millions; at the end of July, to fourteen thousand millions; and the value of one hundred francs in paper fell steadily, first to four francs in gold, then to three, then to two and a half.# But curiously enough, when this depreciation was rapidly going on, as at various other periods when depreciation was rapid, there came an apparent revival of business. ·The hopes of many were revived by the fact that in spite of the decline of paper there was an exceedingly brisk trade in all kinds of permanent property. Whatever articles of permanent value

---

* See Von Sybel, vol. iii, p. 173.

† See Thiers; also, for curious details of measures taken to compel farmers and merchants, see Senior, Lectures on Results of Paper Money, pp. 86, 87.

‡ See Von Sybel, vol. iv, p. 231.

See Von Sybel, vol. iv, p. 330; also tables of depreciation in Moniteur; also official reports in A. D. W. Collection.

certain people were willing to sell, certain other people were willing to buy and pay largely for in assignats. At this, hope revived for a time in certain quarters. But 'ere long it was discovered that this was one of the most terrible results of a natural law which is sure to come into play under such circumstances. It was simply a feverish activity caused by the intense desire of a large number of the shrewder class to convert their paper money into anything and everything which they could hold and hoard until the collapse which they foresaw should take place. This very activity in business was simply the result of disease. It was simply legal robbery of the more enthusiastic and trusting by the more cold-hearted and keen. It was the "unloading" of the assignats by the cunning upon the mass of the people.*

But even this could not stop the madness of inflation. New issues continued, until at the beginning of 1796 over forty-five thousand million francs had been issued, of which over thirty-six thousand millions were in actual circulation.†

---

* For a lifelike sketch of the vigorous way in which these exchanges of assignats for valuable property went on at periods of the rapid depreciation of paper, see Challamel, Les Français sous la Révolution, p. 309; also Say, Économie Politique, septième édition, p. 147.

† See De Nervo, Finances Françaises, p. 280.

It is very interesting to note, in the midst of all this, the steady action of another simple law in finance. The Government, with its prisons and its guillotines, with its laws inflicting twenty years' imprisonment in chains upon the buyers of gold, and death upon investors in foreign securities, was utterly powerless against this law. The *louis d'or* stood in the market as a monitor, noting each day, with unerring fidelity, the decline in value of the assignat; a monitor not to be bribed, not to be scared. As well might the National Convention try to bribe, or scare away, the polarity of the mariner's compass. On August 1, 1795, the gold louis of 25 francs was worth 920 francs; September 1st, 1,200 francs; on November 1st, 2,600 francs; on December 1st, 3,050 francs. In February, 1796, it was worth in market 7,200 francs, or one franc in gold was worth 288 francs in paper money. Prices of all commodities went up in proportion.*

The writings of the period give curious details of these prices. Thibaudeau, in his Memoirs, speaks of sugar as 500 francs a pound, soap 230 francs,

---

* For a very complete table of the depreciation from day to day, see Supplement to the Moniteur, of October 2, 1797. For the market prices of the louis d'or at the first of each month, as the collapse approached, see Montgaillard. See also official lists in the A. D. W. Collection.

candles 140 francs.* Mercier, in his lifelike pictures of the French metropolis at that period, mentions 600 francs as carriage hire for a single drive, and 6,000 francs for an entire day.† Everything was inflated in about the same proportion, except the wages of labor: as manufactories closed, wages had fallen, until all that kept them up at all was the fact that so many laborers were drafted off into the army. From this state of things came grievous wrong and gross fraud. Men who had foreseen these results fully, and had gone into debt, were of course jubilant. He who in 1790 had borrowed 10,000 francs could pay his debts in 1796 for about 35 francs. Laws were made to meet these abuses. As far back as 1794 a plan was devised for publishing official "tables of depreciation" to be used in making equitable settlements of debts, but all such machinery ‡ proved futile. On the 18th of May, 1796, a young man complained to the National Convention that his elder brother, who had been acting as administrator of his deceased father's estate, had paid the heirs in *assignats*, and that he had received scarcely one-three-hundredth part of the real value

---

* See Mémoires de Thibaudeau, vol. ii, p. 26.

† See Le Nouveau Paris, vol. ii, p. 90.

‡ For curious examples of these " scales of depreciation," see the A. D. W. Collection.

of his share.* To meet cases like this, a law was passed establishing a "scale of proportion." Taking as a standard the value of the assignat when there were two billions in circulation, this law declared that, in the payment of debts, one quarter should be added to the amount originally borrowed for every five hundred millions added to the circulation. In obedience to this law a man who borrowed two thousand francs when there were two billions in circulation would have to pay his creditors twenty-five hundred francs when half a billion more was added to the currency, and over thirty thousand francs before the emissions of paper reached their final amount. This brought new evils, worse, if possible, than the old.†

But, widespread as these evils were, they were small compared with the universal distress. The question will naturally be asked, *On whom did this vast depreciation mainly fall, at last?* When this currency had sunk to about one-three-hundredth part of its nominal value, and, after that, to nothing, in whose hands was the bulk of it ? The answer is simple. I will give it in the exact words of that thoughtful historian from whom I have already

---

* For a striking similar case in our own country, see Sumner, History of American Currency, p. 47.

† See Villeneuve Bargemont, Histoire de l'Économie Politique, vol. ii, p. 229.

quoted : " Before the end of the year 1795 the paper money was almost exclusively in the hands of the working classes, employees, and men of small means, whose property was not large enough to invest in stores of goods or national lands.* The financiers and men of large means, though they suffered terribly, were shrewd enough to put much of their property into objects of permanent value. The working classes had no such foresight, or skill, or means. On them finally came the great crushing weight of the loss. After the first collapse came up the cries of the starving. Roads and bridges were neglected ; manufactures were generally given up in utter helplessness." To continue, in the words of the historian already cited : " None felt any confidence in the future in any respect ; none dared to make an investment for any length of time, and it was accounted a folly to curtail the pleasures of the moment, to accumulate or save for an uncertain future." †

While this system was thus running on, a new Government had been established. In October, 1795, came into power the " Directory." It found

---

* See Von Sybel, vol. iv, pp. 337, 338. See, also, for confirmation, Challamel, Histoire Musée, vol. ii, p. 179. For a thoughtful statement of the reasons why such paper was not invested in lands by men of moderate means, and workingmen, see Mill, Political Economy, vol. ii, pp. 81, 82.

† See Von Sybel, vol. iv, p. 222.

the country utterly impoverished, and its only re-
source at first was to print more paper money, and
to issue it even while wet from the press.

The next attempt of the Directory was to secure
a forced loan of six hundred million francs from
the wealthier classes; but this was found fruitless.
Next a national bank was proposed; but capitalists
were loath to embark in banking, while the howls of
the mob against all who had anything especially to
do with money resounded in every city. At last
the Directory bethought themselves of another ex-
pedient. It was by no means new. It was fully
tried on our own continent twice before that time,
and once since—first, in our colonial period; next,
during our Confederation; last, by the recent
"Southern Confederacy"—and here, as elsewhere,
always in vain. But experience yielded to theory—
plain business sense to financial metaphysics. It
was determined to issue a new paper which should
be "fully secured" and "as good as gold."

On February 19, 1796, the copper plates of the
assignats were broken up, and it was decreed that
no more *assignats* be issued; instead of them, it
was decreed that a new paper money, "fully secured, and as good as gold," be issued, under the
name of "*mandats.*" In order that these notes
should be "fully secured," choice public real estate

was set apart to an amount fully equal to the nominal value of the issue, and any one possessing any quantity of the mandats could at once take possession of Government lands to their full face value; the price of the lands to be determined according to their actual rental, and without the formalities and delays previously established in regard to the purchase of lands with assignats. In order to make the mandats "as good as gold," it was planned by forced loans and other means to reduce the quantity of assignats in circulation so that the value of each assignat should be raised to one thirtieth of the value of gold, then to make mandats legal tender, and to substitute them for assignats at the rate of one for thirty.* Never were great expectations more cruelly disappointed. Even before they could be issued from the press, the mandats fell to thirty per cent of their nominal value; from this they speedily fell to fifteen per cent, and soon after to five per cent. This plan failed—just as it failed in New England in 1737; just as it failed under our own Confederation in 1781; just as it failed under the "Southern Confederacy." †

---

* For details of this plan very thoroughly given, see Thiers's History of the French Revolution, Bentley's edition, vol. iv, pp. 410–412.

† For an account of "new tenor bills" and their failure in

To sustain this new currency the Government resorted to every method that ingenuity could devise. Pamphlets were published explaining their advantages to people of every capacity. Never was there more skillful puffing of a financial scheme. A pamphlet, signed "Marchant," and dedicated to "People of Good Faith," was widely circulated. In this Marchant took pains to show the great advantage of the *mandats* as compared with the *assignats:* how land could be more easily acquired with them than with assignats; how their security was better; how they could not by any possibility sink in value as the assignats had done. Even before the pamphlet was dry from the press, the depreciation of mandats had refuted his entire argument.* Then, too, we have at work again the old superstition that there is some way of keeping up the value of paper money other than by having gold ready to redeem as much of it as may be presented. The old plan of penal measures is again pressed. Monot leads off by proposing penalties against those who shall *speak* publicly against the mandats, Talot thinks the penalties ought to be made especially severe; and finally

1737, see Sumner, pp. 27–31; for their failure in 1781, see Morse, Life of Alexander Hamilton, vol. i, pp. 86, 87. For similar failure in Austria, see Sumner, p. 314.

* See Marchant, Lettre aux Gens de Bonne Foi.

it is enacted that any persons "who by their discourse or writing shall decry the *mandats* shall be
condemned to a fine of not less than one thousand
livres, or more than ten thousand; and in case of a
repetition of the offense, to four years in irons." It
was also decreed that those who refuse to receive
the *mandats* be fined the first time the exact sum
which they refuse; the second time, ten times as
much; and the third time, be punished with two
years in prison. But here, too, came in the action
of those natural laws which are alike inexorable in
all countries. This attempt proved futile in France,
just as it had proved futile, less than twenty years
before, in America.* No enactments could stop
the downward tendency of this new paper, "fully
secured," "as good as gold": the laws that finally
govern finance are not made in conventions or con-
gresses.

On July 16, 1796, the great blow was struck. It
was decreed that all paper, *mandats* and *assignats*,
should be taken at its real value, and that bargains
might be made in whatever currency the people
chose. The real value of the mandats at this time
had sunk to about five per cent of their nominal
value.†

---

* See Sumner, p. 44.
† See De Nervo, Finances Françaises, p. 282.

The reign of paper money in France was over. The twenty-five hundred million mandats went into the common heap of refuse with the previous thirty-six billion assignats. The whole vast issue was repudiated.

The collapse had come at last; the whole nation was plunged into financial distress and debauchery from one end to the other.

To this general distress there was, indeed, one exception. In Paris and in a few of the greater cities, men, like Tallien, of the heartless, debauched, luxurious, speculator, contractor, and stock-gambler classes, had risen above the ruins of the multitudes of smaller fortunes. Tallien, one of the worst of the demagogue "reformers," and a certain number of men like him, had been skillful enough to become millionaires, while their dupes, who had clamored for issues of irredeemable paper money, had become paupers.

The luxury and extravagance of these men and their families form one of the most significant features in any picture of the social condition of that period.*

---

* Among the many striking accounts of the debasing effects of "inflation" upon France under the Directory, perhaps the best is that of Lacretelle, vol. xiii, pp. 32–36. For similar effect, produced by same cause in our own country in 1819, see statement from Niles's Register in Sumner, p. 80.

A few years before this the leading women in French society showed a nobleness of character and a simplicity in dress worthy of Roman matrons. Of these were Madame Roland and Madame Desmoulins; but now all was changed. At the head of society stood Madame Tallien, and others like her, wild in extravagance, seeking, daily, new refinements in luxury, and demanding of their husbands and lovers vast sums to array them and feed their whims. If such sums could not be obtained honestly, they must be obtained dishonestly. The more closely one examines that period, the more clearly it is seen that the pictures given by Thibaudeau and Challamel and De Goncourt are not at all exaggerated.*

But when all was over with paper money, specie began to reappear—at first in sufficient sums to do the small amount of business which remained after the collapse. Then, as the business demand increased, the amount of specie flowed in from the world at large to meet it, and the nation gradually recovered from that long paper-money debauch.

Thibaudeau, a very thoughtful observer, tells us in his Memoirs that great fears were felt as to a

---

* For Madame Tallien and luxury of the stock-gambler classes, see Challamel, Les Français sous la Révolution, pp. 30, 33; also De Goncourt, Les Français sous le Directoire.

want of circulating medium between the time when
paper should go out and coin should come in; but
that no such want was ever felt—that coin came in
as if by magic—that the nation rapidly recovered
from its paper-money debauch, and within a year
business entered a new current of prosperity.*

Nothing could better exemplify the saying of
one of the most shrewd of modern statesmen, that
"there will always be money." †

Such, briefly sketched in its leading features, is
the history of the most skillful, vigorous, and per-
sistent attempt ever made to substitute for natural
laws in finance the ability of a legislative body, and
to substitute for a standard of value, recognized
throughout the world, a national standard devised
by theorists and manipulated by schemers. Every
other attempt of the same kind in human history,
under whatever circumstances, has reached similar
results in kind if not in degree; all of them show
the existence in the world of financial laws as sure
in their operation as those laws which hold the
planets in their courses.‡

---

* For similar expectation of a "shock," which did not occur,
at the resumption of specie payments in Massachusetts, see
Sumner, History of American Currency, p. 34.

† See Thiers.

‡ For exemples of similar effects in Russia, Austria, and
Denmark, see Storch, Économie Politique, vol. iv; for similar

I have now presented this history in its chrono-logical order—the order of events: let me, in con-clusion, sum it up in its logical order—the order of causes and effects.

And, first, in the *economic* development. From the first careful issues of paper money, irredeema-ble but moderate, we saw, as an immediate result, apparent improvement and activity in business. Then arose the clamor for more paper money. At first, new issues were made with great difficulty; but, the dike once broken, the current of irredeema-ble currency poured through; and, the breach thus enlarging, this currency was soon swollen beyond control. It was urged on by speculators for a rise in values; by a thoughtless mob, who thought that a nation, by its simple fiat, could stamp real value upon a valueless object: as a consequence, a great debtor class grew rapidly and naturally, and this class gave its influence to depreciate more and more the currency in which its debts were to be paid.*

---

effects in the United States, see Gouge, Paper Money and Bank-ers in the United States; also Sumner, History of American Currency. For working out of the same principles in England, depicted in a masterly way, see Macaulay, History of England, chap. xxi; and for curious exhibition of same causes producing same results in ancient Greece, see a curious quotation by Ma-caulay in same chapter.

* For parallel cases in early history of our own country, see Sumner, p. 21, and elsewhere.

6

All the energy of the Government was devoted to grinding out still more paper; commerce was at first stimulated by the difference in exchange; but this cause soon ceased to operate, and commerce, having been stimulated unhealthfully, wasted away.

Manufactures at first received a great impulse; but, ere long, this overproduction and overstimulus proved as fatal to them as to commerce. From time to time there was a revival of hope by an apparent revival of business; but this revival of business was at last seen to be simply caused by the desire of the more far-seeing and cunning to exchange paper money for objects of permanent value. As to the people at large, the classes living on fixed incomes or salaries felt the pressure first, as soon as the purchasing power of their fixed incomes was reduced. Soon the great class living on wages felt it even more sadly.

Prices of the necessities of life increased; merchants were obliged to increase them, not only to cover depreciation of their merchandise, but also to cover their risk of loss from fluctuation; while the prices of products thus rose, wages, which had gone up at first under the general stimulus, fell. Under the universal doubt and discouragement, commerce and manufactures were checked or destroyed. As a consequence, the demand for labor was stopped;

laboring men were thrown out of employment, and, under the operation of the simplest law of supply and demand, the price of labor—the daily wages of the laboring class—went down until, at a time when prices of food, clothing, and various articles of consumption were enormous, wages were nearly as low as at the time preceding the first issue of irredeemable currency.

The mercantile classes at first thought themselves exempt from the general misfortune. They were delighted at the apparent advance in the value of the goods on their shelves. But they soon found that, as they increased prices to cover the inflation of currency and the risk from fluctuation and uncertainty, purchasers were fewer, purchases less, and payments less sure; a feeling of insecurity spread throughout the country; enterprise was deadened and general stagnation followed.

New issues of paper were clamored for as a new dram is called for by a drunkard. The new issues only increased the evil; capitalists were all the more reluctant to embark their money on such a sea of doubt. Workmen of all sorts were more and more thrown out of employment. Issue after issue of currency came; but no relief save a momentary stimulus, which aggravated the disease. The most ingenious evasions of natural laws in finance which the most subtle theorists could contrive were tried—all in vain; the most brilliant substitutes for those laws were tried; self-regulating schemes, "interconverting" schemes—all equally vain.* All thoughtful men had lost confidence. All men were *waiting;* stagnation became worse and worse. At last came the collapse, and then a return by a fearful shock to a state of things which presented something like certainty of remuneration to capital and labor. Then, and not until then, came the beginning of a new era of prosperity.

Just as dependent on the law of cause and effect was the *moral* development. Out of the inflation of prices grew a speculating class; and, in the complete uncertainty as to the future, all business became a game of chance, and all business men unintentional gamblers. In city centers came a quick growth of stockjobbers and speculators; and these set a debasing fashion in business which spread to the remotest parts of the country. Instead of satisfaction with legitimate gains came admiration for cheatery. Then, too, as values became more and more uncertain, there was no longer any motive for

---

* For a review of some of these attempts, with eloquent statement of their evil results, see Mémoires de Durand de Maillane, pp. 166–169.

care or economy, but every motive for immediate expenditure and present enjoyment. So came upon the nation the *obliteration of the idea of thrift.* In this mania for yielding to present enjoyment rather than providing for future comfort were the seeds of new growths of wretchedness; and luxury, senseless and extravagant, set in: this, too, spread as a fashion. To feed it, there came cheatery in the nation at large, and corruption among officials and persons holding trusts: while the men set such fashions in business, private and official, women like Madame Tallien set fashions of extravagance in dress and living that added to the incentives to corruption. Faith in moral considerations, or even in good impulses, yielded to general distrust. National honor was thought a fiction cherished only by enthusiasts. Patriotism was eaten out by cynicism.

Thus was the history of France logically developed in obedience to natural laws; such has, to a greater or less degree, always been the result of irredeemable paper issues, created according to the whim or interest of legislative assemblies rather than based upon standards of value permanent in their nature and agreed upon throughout the entire commercial world; such, we may fairly expect, will be always the result of them until the fiat of the Almighty shall evolve laws in the universe radically different from those which at present obtain.*

And, finally, as to the general development of the theory and practice which all this history records.

My subject has been Fiat Money in France; How it came; What it brought; and How it ended.

It came by seeking a remedy for a comparatively small evil, in an evil infinitely more dangerous. To cure a disease temporary in its character a corrosive poison was administered which ate out the vitals of French prosperity.

It progressed according to a law in social physics which we may call the *law of accelerating issue and depreciation.* It was comparatively easy to refrain from the first issue; it was exceedingly difficult to refrain from the second ; to refrain from the third and those following was impossible.

It brought, as you have seen, to commerce and manufactures, the mercantile interest, the agricul-

---

* For similar effect of an inflated currency in enervating and undermining trade, husbandry, manufactures, and morals, in our own country, in 1779, see Daniel Webster, cited in Sumner, pp. 45–50. For similar effects in other countries, see Senior, Storch, Macaulay, and others, already cited.

tural interest, utter ruin. It brought on these the
same destruction which would come to a Hollander
opening the dikes of the sea to irrigate his land in a
dry summer.

It ended in the complete financial, moral, and
political prostration of France—a prostration from
which a great absolute monarch alone was able to
draw it.

But this history would be incomplete without a
brief sequel showing how that monarch profited by
this frightful experience. When Bonaparte took
the consulship the condition of fiscal affairs was
appalling. The Government was bankrupt; an
immense debt was unpaid. The further collection
of taxes seemed impossible; the assessments were
in hopeless confusion. War was going on in the
East, on the Rhine, and in Italy, and civil war in
La Vendée. All the armies had been long unpaid,
and the largest loan that could for a moment be
effected was for a sum hardly meeting the expenses
of the Government for a single day. At the first
cabinet council Bonaparte was asked what he in-
tended to do. He replied, "I will pay cash or
pay nothing." From this time he conducted all
his operations on this basis. He arranged the
assessments, funded the debt, and made every payment in cash; and from this time—during all the

campaigns of Marengo, Austerlitz, Jena, Eylau, Friedland, down to the Peace of Tilsit in 1807— there was but one suspension of specie payment, and this only for a few days. When the first great European coalition was formed against the empire, Napoleon was hard pressed financially, and it was proposed to resort to paper money; but he wrote to his minister, "While I live I will never resort to irredeemable paper." He never did, and France under this determination commanded all the gold she needed. When Waterloo came, with the invasion of the allies, with war on her own soil, with a change of dynasty, and heavy expenses for war and indemnities, France, on a specie basis, experienced no severe financial distress.

If we glance at the financial history of France during the Franco-Prussian War and the Communist struggle, in which a far more terrible pressure was brought upon French finance than our own recent civil war put upon American finance, and yet with no national stagnation or distress, but with a steady progress in prosperity, we shall see still more clearly the advantage of meeting a financial crisis in an honest and manly way, and by methods sanctioned by the world's most costly experience, rather than by yielding to the schemes of speculators, or to the dreams of theorists, or to financial metaphysics.*

There is a lesson in all this which it behooves every thinking man to ponder.

---

* For facts regarding French finance under the emperor, I am indebted to Hon. David A. Wells. For more recent triumphs of financial common sense in France, see Bonnet's articles, translated by the late George Walker, Esq.

EFFECTS OF CHEAP COINAGE.

From Macaulay's History of England.

Who suffer the most from the Debasement of the Currency ?—The misgovernment of Charles and James, gross as it had been, had not prevented the common business of life from going steadily and prosperously on. While the honor and independence of the state were sold to a foreign power, while chartered rights were invaded, while fundamental laws were violated, hundreds of thousands of quiet, honest, and industrious families labored and traded, ate their meals, and lay down to rest in comfort and security. Whether Whigs or Tories, Protestants or Jesuits were uppermost, the grazier drove his beasts to market; the grocer weighed out his currants; the draper measured out his broadcloth; the hum of buyers and sellers was as loud as ever in the town; the harvest home was celebrated as joyously as ever in the hamlets;

the cream overflowed the pails of Cheshire; the
apple juice foamed in the presses of Herefordshire;
the piles of crockery glowed in the furnaces of the
Trent, and the barrows of coal rolled fast along the
timber railways of the Tyne.

But when the great instrument of exchange became thoroughly deranged, all trade, all industry,
were smitten as with a palsy. The evil was felt
daily and hourly in almost every place and by
almost every class—in the dairy and on the thrashing
floor, by the anvil and by the loom, on the billows
of the ocean and in the depths of the mine. Nothing could be purchased without a dispute. Over
every counter there was wrangling from morning
to night. The workman and his employer had a
quarrel as regularly as the Saturday came round.
On a fair day or a market day the clamors, the re-
proaches, the taunts, the curses, were incessant; and
it was well if no booth was overturned and no head
broken.

No merchant would contract to deliver goods
without making some stipulation about the quality
of the coin in which he was to be paid. Even men
of business were often bewildered by the confusion
into which all pecuniary transactions were thrown.
The simple and the careless were pillaged without
mercy by extortioners, whose demands grew even

more rapidly than the money shrank.   The price of
the necessaries of life, of shoes, of ale, of oatmeal,
rose fast.   The laborer found that the bit of metal
which, when he received it, was called a shilling
would hardly, when he wanted to purchase a pot of
beer or a loaf of rye bread, go as far as sixpence.
Where artisans of more than usual intelligence were
collected in great numbers, as in the dockyards at
Chatham, they were able to make their complaints
heard and to obtain some redress.   But the ignorant and helpless peasant was cruelly ground between one class which would give money only by
tale and another which would take it only by
weight.

THE END.